AF504390

This book is dedicated to our mothers,
Michelle & Patricia.
Thank you for always inspiring us!

📚 More Adventures Await!

Loved this story? Explore the rest of our magical world! From a garden full of wonder in Grandma Mango, to Switchee the Switch Witch who trades treats for treasures, or a sleepy koala named 'Yawn', and a Boogie Patrol on a mission to the Boogie Bank,
every tale is packed with heart, imagination, and joy.

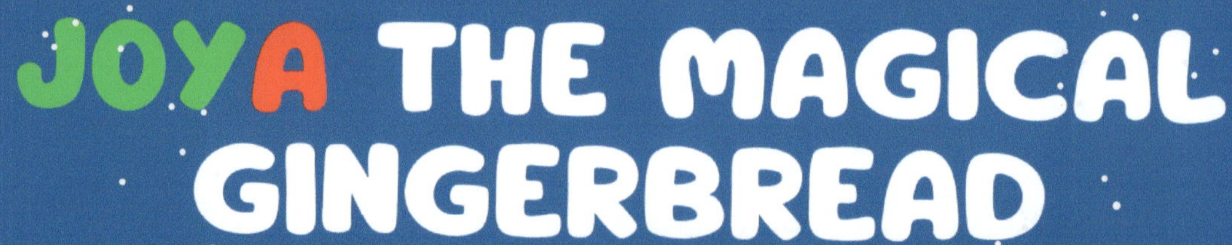

JOYA THE MAGICAL GINGERBREAD

WRITTEN BY: STEPHEN WOOLFOLK
& LINDSAY CHOATE

Once upon a time, in Harmonyville, where snowflakes twinkled and laughter filled the air.

There lived three friends named Martin, Naomi, and Carla who loved Christmas more than anything in the world.

That Christmas Eve, the three friends
sat by the fire, giggling.

But then they remembered something very important. Santa's magic was running low. His sleigh lights were dim, and his reindeer were sleepy.

"If there isn't enough joy," Naomi whispered, "Santa might not reach every home." "We have to help!" said Martin.

"I know!" said Carla.
"Let's make Santa a special cookie full of joy.
"But which one?" asked Martin.
"Gingerbread!", said Naomi.

The children dashed to the kitchen, excitement bubbling inside them. ready to make a special gingerbread cookie filled with love.

They mixed and stirred, adding love and kindness
with every turn.
“Let’s bake gingerbread for Santa every year!”
they cheered.

Naomi, Martin, and Carla carefully placed their creation in the oven and watched with wide eyes as she turned a golden brown.

As the gingerbread baked, they asked, “What should we name her?”

For a moment they were silent, until Naomi whispered, “Joya the Gingerbread.”

The children cheered, "Yay! Joya the Gingerbread!"
The oven went "Beep! Beep!"
"It's time to take her out!"

The children slipped into their cozy Christmas pajamas and snuggled into bed.

Little did they know something magical was about to happen.

As the children drifted off to sleep, Joya the Gingerbread, their favorite gingerbread, came to life!

Joya the Gingerbread blinked her sugary eyes, stretched her cookie arms, and hopped down with a sprinkle of magic.

Joya was made with holiday magic.
Your hugs and family connection bring her to life.
Hug Joya the Gingerbread to activate the magic.

Now it was time. Joya sent her magic out the window, carrying the children's love to help Santa.

The magic grew brighter and brighter, swirling through the night sky until it reached Santa's sleigh.

The sleigh brightened, the reindeer lifted their heads with a jingle, Christmas was saved! Joya the Gingerbread smiled. It worked!

As the sleigh disappeared, Joya the Gingerbread thought of the children. Their love made her real. Now she wanted to thank them.

Joya the Gingerbread tiptoed out of the kitchen to thank the children, leaving tiny cookie crumbs everywhere.

Joya raised her cookie arm. A glowing gingerbread house appeared, bursting open it sent cookies and stickers floating into each stocking.

All was quiet, all was still. Stockings glowed with cookies and stickers, waiting for the children to discover the magic.

As the sun rose, the children shouted,
"We did it!"
"Joya the Gingerbread was here! Look!"

"Joya is real," they whispered.
"She brought us cookies & stickers."
"And our love helped Santa keep
Christmas magic alive."

"Let's bake Joya every Christmas!" they cheered.
And from that day on, the Joya tradition began.

The End

Each Christmas, your family has a mission to carry on this new tradition:

- Bake Joya the Gingerbread with love
- Read her story together
- Let the magic fill your home

More Adventures Await!

Loved this story? Explore the rest of our magical world! From a garden full of wonder in Grandma Mango, to Switchee the Switch Witch who trades treats for treasures, or a sleepy koala named 'Yawn', and a Boogie Patrol on a mission to the Boogie Bank,
every tale is packed with heart, imagination, and joy.

Scan here

Scan here

Scan here

Scan here

www.ingramcontent.com/pod-product-compliance
Lightning Source LLC
Chambersburg PA
CBHW042052100726
47973CB00015B/228
9798330511419